D0894479

# TRAVEL WITH THE GREAT EXPLORERS

Explore with

## Lewis and Clark

**Rachel Stuckey**

Crabtree Publishing Company

www.crabtreebooks.com

# Crabtree Publishing Company

## www.crabtreebooks.com

**Author:** Rachel Stuckey
**Publishing plan research and development:**
   Reagan Miller
**Managing editor:** Tim Cooke
**Editorial director:** Lindsey Lowe
**Editors:** Kelly Spence, Natalie Hyde
**Proofreader:** Kathy Middleton
**Designer:** Lynne Lennon
**Picture manager:** Sophie Mortimer
**Design manager:** Keith Davis
**Children's publisher:** Anne O'Daly
**Production coordinator
      and prepress technican:** Tammy McGarr
**Print coordinator:** Margaret Amy Salter

Produced by Brown Bear Books for
   Crabtree Publishing Company

**Photographs:**
**Front Cover:**
**Robert Hunt Library:** main; **Shutterstock:** Peter Kirillov br;
**Thinkstock:** istockphoto tr. **Topfoto:** The Granger Collection cr.

**Interior: Alamy:** North Wind Picture Archives 15r, 19t, Ron
Niebrugge 17tr, Greg Vaughn 13t: **Art Archive:** Buffalo Bill historical Center, Cody, Wyoming 13 b; **Bridgeman Art Library:**
Private Collection 18-19, Peter Newark American Pictures 21;
**Fort Clatsop Memorial Collection:** 16; **Library of Congress:** 6b,
18, 24, 25, 29; **Mary Evans Picture Library:** 12, Everett
Collection 6t 28tl; **National Archives:** 7; **Public Domain:** 9c, 14;
**Robert Hunt Library:** 8; **Shutterstock:** Neil Hardwick 22r,
Alexey Kamenskiy 10br, M. Niebuhr 22b, Scott E Read 23;
**Thinkstock:** Dorling Kindersley 27, istockphoto 10-11, 11, 17c;
**Topfoto:** The Granger Collection 9t, 20, 26; **Yale University:**
15bl, 28b

### Library and Archives Canada Cataloguing in Publication

Stuckey, Rachel, author
      Explore with Lewis and Clark / Rachel Stuckey.

(Travel with the great explorers)
Includes index.
Issued in print and electronic formats.
ISBN 978-0-7787-1247-3 (bound).--ISBN 978-0-7787-1259-6 (pbk.).--
ISBN 978-1-4271-7574-8 (pdf).--ISBN 978-1-4271-7570-0 (html)

      1. Lewis, Meriwether, 1774-1809--Juvenile literature. 2. Clark,
William, 1770-1838--Juvenile literature. 3. Lewis and Clark Expedition
(1804-1806)--Juvenile literature. 4. Explorers--West (U.S.)--Biography--
Juvenile literature. 5. West (U.S.)--Discovery and exploration--Juvenile
literature. I. Title.

F592.7.S78 2014          j917.804'2          C2013-908705-2
                                             C2013-908706-0

### Library of Congress Cataloging-in-Publication Data

Stuckey, Rachel.
      Explore with Lewis and Clark / Rachel Stuckey.
         pages cm. -- (Travel with the great explorers)
      Includes index.
      ISBN 978-0-7787-1247-3 (reinforced library binding) -- ISBN 978-0-
7787-1259-6 (pbk.) -- ISBN 978-1-4271-7574-8 (electronic pdf) -- ISBN
978-1-4271-7570-0 (electronic html)
      1. Lewis and Clark (1804-1806)--Juvenile literature. 2. West (U.S.)--
Discovery and exploration--Juvenile literature. 3. West (U.S.)--
Description and travel--Juvenile literature. 4. Clark, William, 1770-
1838--Juvenile literature. 5. Lewis, Meriwether, 1774-1809--Juvenile
literature. 6. Explorers--West (U.S.)--Biography--Juvenile literature.
I. Title.

F592.7.S78 2014
917.804'2--dc23
                              2013050839

## Crabtree Publishing Company

www.crabtreebooks.com  1-800-387-7650

Printed in the USA/092016/JF20160816

**Published in Canada
Crabtree Publishing**
616 Welland Ave.
St. Catharines, ON
L2M 5V6

**Published in the United States
Crabtree Publishing**
PMB 59051
350 Fifth Avenue, 59th Floor
New York, New York 10118

**Published in the United Kingdom
Crabtree Publishing**
Maritime House
Basin Road North, Hove
BN41 1WR

**Published in Australia
Crabtree Publishing**
3 Charles Street
Coburg North
VIC, 3058

# CONTENTS

# Meet the Bosses

Famous explorers Lewis and Clark came from very different backgrounds, but were old friends from the U.S. army. They were hired by President Thomas Jefferson to explore the new American territory.

## AYE-AYE, CAPTAIN!

+ President's right-hand man

+ Trained on the frontier

Meriwether Lewis (1774–1809) was a captain in the U.S. Army. Born in Virginia, he lived on the Georgia frontier, but at the age of 13 returned to Virginia to study. After serving in the army, Lewis acted as Thomas Jefferson's personal secretary. That was one reason the President asked him to lead the expedition.

## A HANDY MAN

☛ Veteran learns practical skills

☛ Former spy works for government

William Clark (1770–1838) was another Virginian, but, unlike Lewis, he had no formal education. He learned useful skills serving on the Kentucky and Ohio frontiers in the U.S. Army, which he joined at the age of 19. He was even sent to spy on the Spanish. Clark became an army captain in 1795, but retired the following year.

# OH CAPTAIN, MY CAPTAIN!

## ★ Explorer denied rank by U.S. Army

In 1795, when Lewis was in the army, he served under Captain Clark. The two became friends. When Lewis was picked for the expedition, he asked his friend to lead it with him. But the army gave Clark the lower rank of second lieutenant, not captain. Lewis decided it didn't matter. He always referred to Clark as captain in front of their men.

## My Explorer Journal

★ **Imagine you are on the expedition. What difference might it make if you knew that William Clark was only a second lieutenant, not a captain? Would you still pay as much attention to him?**

" To explore the Missouri River and such principal stream of it as by its course and communication with the waters of the Pacific … the most direct and practicable water communication across this continent." *Thomas Jefferson outlines the purpose of the expedition.*

# THE THIRD PRESIDENT

## + Jefferson's vision of the country

Thomas Jefferson was author of the **Declaration of Independence**. When he was elected president in 1801, France controlled the heart of North America, including the Mississippi River. Britain controlled the Oregon Territory and Canada, and Spain controlled much of the Southwest. Jefferson bought the Louisiana Territory from France. With competitors for the land on all sides, he had to work quickly to claim it.

## Did you know?

The Louisiana Purchase of 1803 more than doubled the size of the United States.

# Where Are We Heading?

In 1803, the United States bought the Louisiana Territory from France. Almost one-third of the country's present size, it doubled the size of the United States at the time. Lewis and Clark were sent to explore it.

## MAKE IT PLAIN

☞ **Explorers find endless grassland**

☞ **Farmland at the heart of the continent**

The Great Plains stretch from the Mississippi in the east, south into Mexico, to the Rocky Mountains in the west, and north into Canada. The plains make up about half a million square miles of North America. Today the Great Plains are important for farming and ranching. The tall grasses and wild animal herds Lewis and Clark saw there have almost disappeared.

## CONTINENTAL DIVIDE

★ **Mountains split the country in two**

The Rocky Mountains are one of the world's largest mountain ranges. In 1803, Americans knew they were there, but had no idea how high they were and how much ground they covered. The Rockies mark the point where the continent's rivers divide. On one side, they flow east, toward the Atlantic Ocean; on the other side they flow west toward the Pacific Ocean. The explorers followed the Columbia River from the Rockies to the sea.

### Sensation

President Jefferson believed North America was home to volcanoes erupting with fire, mountains of salt—and woolly mammoths.

# TRAVEL UPDATE

## Beautiful coastline

★The Pacific Coast has many beaches, a mild climate, mountain ranges, and dense forests. It has natural harbors for ports and fertile land for farming. But with most of the coast controlled by Spain, the only way to get there before 1803 was by sea—and the voyage took over six months.

> **I do not believe that there is in the universe a similar extent of country equally fertile and well watered."** *Lewis, about the Missouri Valley*

## My Explorer Journal

★ The crew of the expedition, called the Corps of Discovery, saw many wonders on their journey. Use one of these pictures to write a journal entry describing what you see—and why it might be useful to the United States.

## MIGHTY MISSOURI

**+ River to the west**

Lewis and Clark began their journey by following the Missouri River to its source in the Rocky Mountains. The river flows over 2,300 miles (3,700 km) east across the Great Plains to the Mississippi River near St. Louis, from where they set out. The **elevation** of the river in the Rockies is almost 2 miles (3 km) above sea level.

# Lewis and Clark's Route across North America

Lewis and Clark set off from St. Louis with their crew, the Corps of Discovery, in May 1804, to find a river route to the Pacific Ocean. They reached the ocean in November 1805. In March 1806, they set off for home, arriving back in St. Louis late that September.

**Washington (modern)**

**Columbia River**

**Oregon (modern)**

**Idaho (modern)**

**Montana (modern)**

**Wyoming (modern)**

**LOUISIANA PURCHASE**

**NEW SPAIN (SPANISH TERRITORY)**

## Fort Clatsop
All of the Corps of Discovery voted on where to spend the winter of 1805–1806. They built a "fort" of two separate huts. The winter was wet and miserable. When spring finally came, they stole a canoe from the Clatsop Indians and headed back up the Columbia River.

## Bitterroot Mountains
The explorers nearly starved crossing the Bitterroots in winter. On the other side of the mountains, the Nez Perce tribe gave them food. They also told the Corps how to float to the Pacific Ocean down the Clearwater, Snake, and Columbia Rivers.

## Great Falls
The expedition had to carry their boats and supplies around the Great Falls of the Missouri River, now in Montana. The mighty falls ended their hope that there might be a continuous water route all the way to the Pacific Ocean.

**Scale**
0          400 km

400 miles

## Rocky Mountains

On the return journey, the Corps split up so that they could explore the two main **tributaries** of the Missouri River, including the Yellowstone and Marias rivers. They reunited after a few weeks.

## Fort Mandan

The expedition spent the winter of 1804–05 near the Mandan and Hidatsa villages in what is now North Dakota. They built a fort where they wrote reports about their journey so far.

**Nova Scotia**

**CANADA (BRITISH TERRITORY)**

**Fort Mandan**

**North Dakota (modern)**

**South Dakota (modern)**

**Great Lakes**

**Indiana Territory**

**Missouri River**

**Nebraska (modern)**

## St. Louis

The expedition set out from St. Louis, Missouri, the largest city in the West. When they returned 28 months later, they had traveled nearly 8,000 miles (13,000 km). Most people believed they were dead.

**UNITED STATES**

**Locator map**

**St. Louis**

**Missouri (modern)**

### Key

→ Outward Journey

→ Homeward Journey

·····▶ Lewis

------▶ Clark

# Meet the Corps

Lewis and Clark selected more than 30 volunteers for their skills, experience, and character. They formed the Corps of Discovery, a special branch of the United States Army.

## Guide

Sacagawea had traveled widely. She used natural features such as rock formations to tell the Captains which way to go.

## Native Guide

☞ **Enslaved Woman Joins Expedition**

☞ **Fur Trader Brings Along His Wife**

Sacagawea is the most famous member of the Corps. She was a native Shoshone who had been captured and enslaved as a young girl by the Hidatsa, a warring tribe. She later married a French-Canadian fur trader named Toussaint Charbonneau, who was hired by Lewis and Clark because he had lived among native people in North Dakota for years. When the Captains learned about Sacagawea's past, they realized she might be a useful guide.

## BABY WALKER

**+ Have You Got the Travel Cot?**

Sacagawea's baby son, Jean-Baptiste, spent the first two years of his life on the expedition. William Clark nicknamed him Little Pomp. A sandstone formation on the Yellowstone River was named Pompey's Pillar for him.

# RIGHT-HAND MAN

### + The Captains' Main Advisor

George Droulliard was half French and half Shawnee Indian. He was paid five times as much as the other men. He was an excellent hunter and knew Indian sign language. He often went with Lewis on scouting trips.

## Did you know?

Only one animal made the round trip with the Corps. Seaman was a black labrador dog that Lewis bought before the start of the trip.

# NOT A VOLUNTEER

★ **African-American Pioneer**

★ **Unique Talent**

York was Captain Clark's manservant. He was a slave who had grown up alongside Clark. York was the first African the native people had ever seen. He also had a special skill: unlike most of the Corps, York could swim.

## My Explorer Journal

★ **The members of the Corps had to be tough enough to face hardship and danger. Write a letter to Lewis and Clark explaining why you'd be a good recruit and why you'd like to join their expedition.**

# LOST IN TRANSLATION

★ **Does Anyone Speak Shoshone?**

Some of the Corps were French-Canadian fur **trappers**. Others were the children of European fathers and native women. They helped the Captains to communicate. With the Shoshone, for example, the Captains spoke English, which the French-Canadians translated into French. Charbonneau turned the French to Hidatsa, and Sacagawea translated Hidatsa into Shoshone.

# Check Out the Ride

Because Lewis and Clark followed the Missouri River and were looking for a river route to the Pacific Ocean, the Corps of Discovery traveled most of the way by boat.

## AGAINST THE CURRENT

☞ Sailing Upstream

☞ Shifting Heavy Loads

> " I recollected the folly of the attempt I was about to make, which was to throw myself into the river and endeavour to swim to the pirogue." *Meriwether Lewis describes the sinking of one of the Corps' pirogues.*

The Missouri River flows from west to east, so the Corps traveled against the current on the first part of their journey. They used two kinds of boat. Keelboats are large and flat-bottomed. A keel, or blade, runs underneath the length of the boat to stabilize it. The keelboat was 55 feet (17 m) long and 8 feet (2.5 m) wide and could carry 10 tons (10.2 metric tons) of supplies. Pirogues were large canoes, with room for eight rowers and supplies.

## RIVER CRAFT

+ Men who know the Missouri

+ A Difficult Trip

**Did you know?**

Pulling the boats could be tough. Rocks in the rivers could cut the boatmen's feet or make them fall in the water.

The Captains hired experienced boatmen to help them. The boatmen would paddle and row, directed by a **pilot**, who steered the boat. Sometimes they used poles to push along the bottom of the river. In shallow water, they even waded in the river and pulled the boats by rope. It was a difficult trip!

# TRAVEL UPDATE

## Going Overland

★When traveling by boat, sooner or later you have to get out and walk—either to get around rapids or a waterfall, or to move from one body of water to another. Carrying canoes over land is called portaging. At the Great Falls of the Missouri River the Corps had to carry all of their boats and supplies 18 miles (28 km). The portage took a whole month!

# RIDE 'EM COWBOY

★ Let's use Horsepower

★ Four Legs is Better than Two

When they reached the mountains, Lewis and Clark met the Shoshone. Thanks to Sacagawea, who was a Shoshone, the people loaned the Corps horses. The men used the animals to travel up and over the Rocky Mountains, where they met the Nez Perce tribe.

# LIKE FALLING OFF A LOG

☞ Using Indian Technology

Once the Corps crossed the Rockies, they traveled by river again. The ridge of the Rockies served as the **Continental Divide**, so now all the rivers flowed west! The Nez Perce showed the Corps how to make canoes from hollowed-out tree trunks. Now moving in the same direction as the current, they floated down the Clearwater, Snake, and Columbia rivers to the Pacific.

# Solve It with Science

Some of Lewis and Clark's most important supplies on the expedition were scientific tools. They used these tools to navigate and make maps and records as they went.

## APPLIANCE OF SCIENCE

☛ Explorers Use the Latest Gadgets

☛ You're Never Lost with a Compass

### Pioneers

The Captains were not the first people to map the heart of North America. Many native people drew accurate maps on birch bark or on rocks.

The Captains had various scientific tools to study the territory through which they passed. A compass showed the direction they were heading, and a thermometer gave an accurate temperature. They used a telescope to see far distances on land and to study the position of the stars. By studying the heavens and using their chronometer—a highly accurate clock—to tell the precise time, they could work out their **longitude**, or how far west they had traveled.

## SURVEYING

★ I Came, I Saw...I Drew a Map

Jefferson wanted the Captains to make a precise map of their journey. Lewis used **surveyor's** tools to measure distances, elevation, and longitude and **latitude**. **Sextants** measured the angles of mountain peaks so their height could be calculated. **Quadrants** allowed the Corps to tell the time using the position of the sun. The Corps used logs tied to lines to measure the speed of river currents.

# WHAT CLASS ARE YOU IN?

+ Scientific approach to nature

+ Studying new species

Meriwether Lewis had a life-long interest in natural history. He grew up hunting in the woods, and his mother taught him to collect plants to be used as medicines. He and Clark identified many new species of flora and fauna, or plants and animals. They sketched samples in their journals and took specimens back east to be cataloged and classified. This was the first glimpse most Americans had of the natural riches of their new western "wilderness."

## My Explorer Journal

★ **Imagine you are an explorer in a new place. Use a ruler and some string for measuring, and draw a map of your bedroom or another room in your home.**

## Did you know?

The maps drawn by Lewis and Clark were the most accurate available in the United States for many decades.

# SHOWING OFF

☛ **One man's magic is another man's science**

As part of their mission to make friends with the native people they met, the Corps of Discovery used science to impress and entertain their new friends. They showed off with magnets and shot targets with an air gun. This seemed like magic to the native people who had no such tools themselves.

# Hanging at Home

The Corps were away for over two years. They lived in tents or built themselves shelters they called "forts." There was lots to eat and plenty of work or distractions to help pass the time.

## Trade

The Mandan traded with the Corps at Fort Mandan. The native people exchanged food for items such as glass beads.

## LIVING OFF THE LAND

☛ Meat, Meat, and More Meat...

☛ Has Anyone Seen any Salad?

The Corps of Discovery was often surrounded by herds of buffalo, elk, and deer. But Lewis wrote in his journal that "altho' game is very abundant and gentle, we only kill as much as is necessary for food." Eating too much meat upset the stomachs of many of the men. Sacagawea picked edible wild plants to improve their diets.

## A WINTER HOME
★ Wooden fortress—with NO modern conveniences

The Corps of Discovery spent their first winter in North Dakota among the Mandan and Hidatsa people. They built a shelter called Fort Mandan after their new neighbors. The triangular fort was built from cottonwood lumber, with a gate on the side facing the Missouri River.

# TRAVEL UPDATE

## Are you sure it's got 4 stars?

★After spending over a year reaching the Pacific coast, the Corps needed a place to stay. Fort Clatsop, near the mouth of the Columbia River, was ideal. It took three weeks to build in rainy weather, and was finished on Christmas Day 1805. There were two buildings: one for the men and the other for Sacagawea's family and the Captains.

## ALL TIED UP

☞ Give them enough rope

The Corps spent much of their time making rope by twisting together fibers of hemp or thin strips of bear or elk skin. On the river, rope was used to tie sails; it was used to drag boats over portages; it made bridles, or leads, for horses; and it anchored tents to the ground.

 **Weather Forecast**

## ANYONE GOT AN UMBRELLA?

"The weather forecast for Fort Clatsop is rain. Tomorrow looks like more rain. And the day after that. And the next." The Corps spent a miserable, boring winter in the cool, damp climate of the Pacific Northwest.

## A WHALE OF EXCITEMENT

★ Let's go see the monster

At Fort Clatsop, the Corps learned from a native visitor that a whale had died on a nearby beach. Two of the men saw it while collecting salt from the ocean and brought back some whale meat. The others cooked and ate it. Then a small group went by boat to see the "monster" and bring back more meat and **blubber** to make oil. But after this excitement, it was a long and boring winter for the men.

> I had a part of it cooked and found it very palatable and tender. It resembled the beaver or the dog in flavour." *Lewis on first tasting whale meat.*

# Our New Friends

## WELCOME TO OUR VILLAGE

★ **Explorers trade food and knowledge**

The Mandan lived in villages on the Missouri River, where they farmed corn, beans, and squash. They also hunted buffalo during an annual hunt. They had been trading with Europeans for a long time and welcomed Lewis and Clark, who spent their first winter with the Mandan. Both the Mandan and the neighboring Hidatsa gave the explorers a lot of information about the territory to the west.

### Kidnap!

Sacagawea was kidnapped at the age of about 12 during a raid on the Shoshone by the Hidatsa. A year later she was sold to Charbonneau as his wife.

## Native-American stereotypes!

☛ **It's not all tipis and feathers!**

The Lakota, or the Teton Sioux, were semi-**nomadic** hunters who lived in what is now South Dakota. Lewis and Clark met them in September of 1804. Some things often associated with all Native Americans actually relate to the Lakota, such as tipis and headdresses. The Lakota originally tried to prevent the Corps from traveling up the Missouri River, but changed their minds because they wanted European goods to trade with their neighbors, the Arikara, for food.

# HARD TIMES

+ Shoshone driven from the plains

+ Sacagawea welcomed home

The Shoshone hunted buffalo on the plains until neighboring tribes got guns from the Spanish and British. These tribes then began to raid the Shoshone. The Shoshone moved to the base of the Rockies. Life was harder there, and they lived on wild plants, fish, and small animals. Despite their less than plentiful lifestyle, they happily shared their food with the Corps, and gave them horses and information about crossing the mountains.

> " The most hospitable, honest and sincere people that we have met with in our voyage."
> *Lewis describes the Nez Perce.*

# MISTAKEN IDENTITY

★ Explorer mix-up

★ Flatheads don't have flat heads

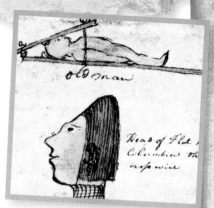

Lewis and Clark named the people who lived between the Rockies and the Cascade Mountains the Flathead, because they thought they had flattened brows. The Flathead called themselves Salish. Although some Salish peoples strapped hard boards to children's heads to flatten their brows, the group Lewis and Clark met did not actually do so.

# NOSE JOB

☞ Why aren't your noses pierced?

When Lewis and Clark crossed the Rockies, they met the Nez Perce. The tribe's name comes from the French words for "pierced nose." In fact, it was the nearby Chinook tribe that pierced their noses. The Nez Perce helped the Corps find food after they had crossed the mountains. And when the Corps moved on by boat, they left their horses with the tribe for safekeeping.

# Meeting and Greeting

While they were away, the expedition made contact with almost 50 different native nations. Although there were a few problems, most of the encounters were peaceful.

> "We sent for some chiefs of that nation to let them know of the change of government and the wishes of our government to cultivate friendship with them."
> *William Clark describes meeting the Otos.*

## WE MEAN NO HARM

**+ Explorers encourage trade**

**+ Linking hands across America**

Lewis and Clark had both lived on the frontier and met native people. They wanted to be fair in their dealings with them. Before the expedition began, Lewis hosted a council between members of the Oto and Missouri Indians. The experience helped to shape Lewis and Clark's approach to meeting people from new cultures.

## Meet the President!

☛ **Explorers hand out medals**

☛ **Signs of peace**

Lewis and Clark took about 90 medals to present to the chiefs they met. These peace medals had an engraving of Jefferson on one side and a handshake on the other. Jefferson wanted the United States to make the native peoples allies, so he invited native chiefs to Washington, D.C. But he was also eager to claim **sovereignty** over the land.

# HELLO, LITTLE SISTER

- Family reunion for Sacagawea
- Shoshone welcome back kidnap victim

In August of 1805, Lewis led a scouting party that first met with the Shoshone. Lewis worried about how to obtain horses from the tribe. But when Clark and the rest of the Corps arrived in the camp, they were all surprised to learn that the Chief waiting to meet them was Cameahwait, Sacagawea's brother. The two were very happy to see each other again, and the Captains had no trouble trading for their horses.

## My Explorer Journal

★ Some native people were suspicious of the Corps, while others were friendly. Imagine you belonged to a tribe who met the Corps. How do you think you would react? Give reasons to explain your decision.

## Reunion

Sacagawea was so overjoyed to meet her brother again that she kept having to stop translating because she was crying with joy.

# HELLO NEIGHBOR

★ First encounters between peoples

★ Delicate diplomacy

As Lewis and Clark traveled farther west, they met many Indians who had never seen a white person before. Communication was difficult and there were many misunderstandings. The Corps did not understand the leadership structures and trade practices of the different groups, or their relationships with one another. Some groups were afraid of the newcomers. Others were friendly and welcoming. Some paid the small band little attention.

## Did you know?

While the Corps was in the West, Jefferson welcomed Missouri, Oto, Arikara, and Yangton Sioux chiefs to the White House.

# I Love Nature

One of the tasks Jefferson gave Lewis and Clark was to catalog the natural resources of the West. He thought they might even meet woolly mammoths!

## Horrible

The Corps encountered the grizzly bear, whose scientific name is *Ursus horribilis*—the horrible bear!

## MEETING NEW SPECIES

☛ **Natural wonders of the West**

☛ **A present for the President**

The Corps of Discovery identified more than 300 species of plants and animals unknown to Europeans—but no mammoths. In their journals the Captains described prairie dogs, pronghorn antelope, and other new species. They collected samples of plants, such as sagebrush. When a small party returned from the expedition early, they sent live specimens back to Washington, D.C. They included a prairie dog as a gift for Jefferson.

## Did you know?

Meriwether Lewis drew a picture of a eulachon, a small fish some native peoples ate. He said it was "lussious"—luscious, or delicious.

## WHAT'S IN A NAME?

★ **Scientific names remember explorers**

Cutthroat Trout has a distinctive red jaw. Its scientific name is *Oncorhynchus clarki*. It was named in honor of Clark, who carefully drew the fish in his journal. Lewis's Woodpecker, or *Melanerpes lewis,* is one of the largest species of American woodpecker and was also named for the explorer who described it so well.

★ **Imagine that you are one of the explorers and that you are writing to tell President Jefferson about the new animals you have found. How would you describe a grizzly bear to someone who has never seen one? Or a prairie dog?**

# THE BIG THREE

## ★ Watch out for that bear

In the expedition's journals, the three most talked-about animals are the beaver, the buffalo, and the grizzly bear. The rivers were full of beaver. They had drawn fur traders farther west. The buffalo roamed the plains and were hunted by many people. But, by far, the grizzly bear was the most ferocious animal the Corps had ever seen.

# LEWIS THE NATURALIST

## + Explorer turns scientist!

Although he had no formal training, Meriwether Lewis was a talented **naturalist**. He was very good at noticing details others overlooked. He knew how to use scientific **taxonomy** for classifying living things. This system gave each species a name made up from two Latin words. He also wrote long detailed accounts describing the things he saw so that other naturalists could learn about them.

 **Weather Forecast**

# WACKY WEATHER

Lewis and Clark experienced different weather on their trip. They noted snowfall on the Plains in the spring and fall, but warm winters at the Pacific coast. They suffered through hailstorms and flash floods. They carefully recorded the temperature twice a day—until their last thermometer broke!

# Fortune Hunting

Jefferson did not send Lewis and Clark off across North America just out of curiosity. He was eager for the explorers to find things that would benefit the economy of the United States.

## Blocked

The rivers to northern Canada and the Arctic Ocean were frozen for much of the year. A Northwest Passage through the North would have been of little use for trade.

## Use It or Lose It

- Let's get there first!
- Colonial competition for land

One reason for exploring the heart of the continent was so they could lay claim to it. The United States had bought the Louisiana Territory from the French, but Spain still controlled the land to the west and south of the area. Great Britain had the territories to the north and west. Until the Americans explored the territory there was little to stop other countries from gradually moving in and taking parts of it.

## TRAVEL UPDATE

### New route to the West Coast

★ You have two ways to get from the east coast to the west coast. Before 1803, the only choice was to sail down the Atlantic coast of North and South America, around Cape Horn, and then up the Pacific coast. The journey takes over six months this way. But now you can take Lewis and Clark's cross-country route along rivers and across the Rocky Mountains. What's your preference?

# THE NORTHWEST PASSAGE

★ **No through-route to Asia**

★ **No commercial benefits found**

Jefferson hoped Lewis and Clark might find the legendary Northwest Passage—a water route to the Pacific Ocean and Asia. In fact, the Great Falls of the Missouri River and the Rocky Mountains put an end to that possibility. Later explorers found more practical ways of traveling west. It turned out there really is a Northwest Passage, but it is in the far north at the top of Canada. No one traveled the route successfully until 1906!

### Did you know?

Jefferson hoped to discover a river route to the far north. That would give the United States control of trade with northern Canada—the richest source of furs.

# FUR FRENZY

☛ **Fashions drive exploration**

☛ **Beaver hats are all the rage**

One of the most profitable resources of the West was fur. Since the 1700s, young adventurers from the European colonies had hunted beaver for fur or traded with the native people for pelts. By the 1800s, the fur trade was dominated by the British and French-Canadians. The Louisiana Purchase gave Americans a chance to break into the **lucrative** business. Many trappers followed Lewis and Clark into the wilderness—and became explorers themselves.

One way to increase trade was to improve relationships with the people who knew the territory best. This was one reason friendship with native tribes was important to Jefferson. He believed that **prosperity** for the United States depended on avoiding war with the inhabitants already living in the new territory.

# MAKING FRIENDS

+ **President prefers peace to war**

+ **Explorers establish friendly contact**

# This Isn't What It Said in the Brochure!

Over the two-year expedition, many things went wrong. There was bad weather, then food shortages, hostile people, and dangerous animals. Of course, for many native people, this was their everyday life.

## MUDDY WATERS

- Don't drink the water
- And don't fall in!

**Did you know?**

One pirogue, or canoe, sank with many of the expedition's valuable notes. After this loss, Meriwether Lewis said he was plunged into despair.

Traveling by river brought its own difficulties. Many men grew sick from dysentery. Clark believed the illness was caused by the muddy river water, which they drank. He may have been right. Dysentery is an intestinal infection caused by bacteria found in dirty water. The river also presented another danger. Boats could easily overturn—and few of the Corps could swim.

## "MOSQUITOES ARE TROUBLESOME"

★ Bug alert!
★ Even the dog gets attacked!

The bugs were very bad. There were clouds of mosquitoes and ticks all along the Missouri River. Sacagawea's son, Little Pomp, was bitten so badly his face swelled up. Sometimes the mosquitoes made it impossible to hunt, cook, or make camp. Even Seaman, the dog, was tortured by the bugs.

# FEROCIOUS ENCOUNTERS

**+ Don't feed the animals**

In Montana, expert hunter George Drouillard killed a grizzly bear that was threatening the Corps. The Captains were shocked to note that it was bigger than any animal they had ever seen. Wolves were another threat. In his journal, Clark describes peering into a den of wolf pups. He was very lucky the pups' mother didn't see him. Wolves would attack anyone threatening their pups.

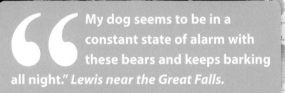

> **My dog seems to be in a constant state of alarm with these bears and keeps barking all night."** *Lewis near the Great Falls.*

## My Explorer Journal

★ **The Corps of Discovery faced many hardships, but they didn't give up. What would have been the most difficult part of the journey for you? How do you think you would overcome the difficulty?**

# SINGLE FATALITY

☞ **Only one man lost**

Despite all the dangers, only one member of the Corps of Discovery died—and not how you might expect. Only three months into the expedition, Sergeant Charles Floyd's appendix ruptured, or burst. No one could help him, and eventually he died.

**Weather Forecast**

## SUFFERING IN THE BITTERROOTS

As the Corps crossed the Bitterroot Mountains, temperatures fell below freezing. At night it was even colder. Lewis said it was the coldest he had ever been. They lost their way in the snow. The mountains took far longer to cross than anyone expected.

# End of the Road

The Corps arrived back in St. Louis on September 23, 1806—two years and four months after they left. Most people thought they were dead, so there were huge celebrations on their return.

## RETURN JOURNEY

- Home in only SIX months
- An easier journey back

In March 1806, the Corps of Discovery left the Pacific coast and headed up the Columbia River in two canoes. After crossing the Bitterroot Mountains again, Lewis and Clark split the Corps into two groups to explore more territory. They met up again at the Yellowstone River. They traveled quickly down the Missouri River, sometimes covering 70 miles (110 km) in a day!

## JOB WELL DONE

★ Credit where credit is due

In 1807, Lewis wrote to the Secretary of War about the men of the Corps of Discovery: "The patience and fortitude with which they submitted to, and bore, the fatigues and painful sufferings incident to my late tour to the Pacific Ocean, entitles them to my warmest **approbation** and thanks."

# JUST REWARDS

+ What the Corps did next

+ Heading back to the West

Lewis and Clark became national heroes and went to many parties in their honor. As Lewis suggested, the men of the Corps were awarded double pay and 320 acres (129 hectares) of land each. But many, like John Colter, stayed in the West to work as guides and fur traders. Lewis and Clark were given important positions in the government, as well as 1,600 acres (647 hectares) of land each.

## WHAT BECAME OF SACAGAWEA?

☛ Living among the Mandan

☛ Pompey travels to Europe

On the way home, Sacagawea stayed at the Mandan villages with Charbonneau, who worked as a guide on the frontier. In 1808, the couple visited St. Louis. They left their son with Clark, who paid for his education. Pompey, whose real name was Jean-Baptiste, became a fur trapper and guide. He even traveled to Europe at the invitation of a German prince! His mother is believed to have died living among the Mandan in 1812.

## The End

The Captains offered to take Charbonneau and his family to St. Louis, but the trapper refused. He said he would not be able to make a living there.

## THE CAPTAINS

+ Conflicting fortunes

The Captains had different experiences after their journey. Meriwether Lewis became the governor of the Louisiana Territory, but never got used to working in an office. He was accused of trying to split Louisiana from the United States before he died in 1809. William Clark became brigadier general of the Louisiana militia and was later governor of the Missouri Territory. He supported U.S. expansion in the West, but was known for his compassion and respect for native culture.

### My Explorer Journal

★ The President was so pleased with the Corps that he doubled their pay and gave them land. Why do you think some of the men chose to go back into the West to live?

# GLOSSARY

**approbation** Approval or praise

**blubber** The fat of whales and other sea creatures which is used to produce oil

**Continental Divide** The line that defines the direction in which water flows between the Atlantic and Pacific Oceans in North America

**Declaration of Independence** The document signed in 1776 declaring the independence of the United States from Britain as a country

**economy** The process of producing, selling, and buying goods in a country or region

**elevation** The height of something

**fertile** Able to grow plants such as crops in great abundance

**latitude** How far a location on Earth is north or south of the equator

**longitude** How far a location on Earth is to the east or west of an imaginary line passing through Greenwich in London

**lucrative** Describes something that is very profitable

**naturalist** Someone who studies plants and animals

**nomadic** A person or group who moves from one place to another

**Northwest Passage** A sea route between Europe and East Asia through the Arctic Ocean around the top of North America

**palatable** Edible or pleasant to eat

**pilot** A sailor who steers a vessel, often in dangerous waters

**prosperity** Being successful and thriving

**quadrants** Navigational devices used to measure the altitude of heavenly bodies above the horizon

**rapids** Part of a river where the current is so fast and turbulent that vessels cannot travel through

**sextants** Navigational devices used to measure the altitude of heavenly bodies above the horizon

**sovereignty** The formal control of an area

**surveyor** Someone who studies the geographical features of land

**taxonomy** The science of identifying, describing, naming, and classifying species

**trappers** People who trap wild animals for their fur

**tributaries** Streams that flow into a larger stream or body of water

**JANUARY** President Jefferson proposes to Congress an expedition to explore the Missouri River.

**MAY 14** The Corps of Discovery leaves St. Louis to travel up the Missouri River.

**APRIL 7** A small group returns to St. Louis with maps and specimens; the others continue up the Missouri.

**JUNE 13** The Corps arrives at the Great Falls of the Missouri. Lewis calls it "the grandest sight I ever beheld."

**1803**

**1804**

**1805**

**MAY** The United States buys Louisiana from the French, doubling the size of the country.

**OCTOBER** The Corps arrives at the Mandan and Hidatsa villages in what is now North Dakota and built Fort Mandan to spend the winter.

**JULY 4** The two-week portage of the Great Falls is completed. The Corps celebrates Independence Day by dancing into the night.

# ON THE WEB

**www.pbs.org/lewisandclark/**
Extensive PBS site created to accompany the Ken Burns' movie *Lewis and Clark: The Journey of the Corps of Discovery.*

**www.nationalgeographic.co.uk/lewisandclark/**
National Geographic site with an interactive log of the expedition.

**http://lewis-clark.org/**
Discovering Lewis and Clark site maintained by the Lewis and Clark Fort Mandan Foundation.

**www.lewisandclarkexhibit.org/index_flash.html**
Online national exhibition put together to celebrate the bicentennial of Lewis and Clark's journey.

# BOOKS

Crompton, Samuel Willard. *Lewis and Clark* (Great Explorers). Chelsea House Publishers, 2009.

Fradin, Judith Bloom, and Dennis Brindell Fradin. *The Lewis and Clark Expedition* (Turning Points in U.S. History). Benchmark Books, 2007.

Frazier, Neta Lohnes. *Path to the Pacific: The Story of Sacajawea.* Sterling Point, 2008.

Hamen, Susan E. *The Lewis and Clark Expedition* (Essential Events). Abdo Publishing Company, 2008.

Robinson, Kate. *Lewis and Clark: Exploring the American West* (Great Explorers of the World). Enslow Publishers Ltd, 2010.

Rodger, Ellen. *Lewis and Clark: Opening the American West* (In the Footsteps of Explorers). Crabtree Publishing Company, 2005.

Schanzer, Rosalyn. *How We Crossed the West: The Adventures of Lewis and Clark.* National Geographic Children's Books, 2012.

---

**AUGUST**
The Corps meet a Shoshone band led by Sacagawea brother, Cameahwait.

**OCTOBER 18**
The Corps reach the Columbia River, having descended the Clearwater and Snake Rivers.

**JULY 3**
The Expedition divides into groups to explore; they are reunited some three weeks later.

**SEPTEMBER 23**
The Corps of Discovery receives a heroes' welcome on their return to St. Louis.

**1806**

**SEPTEMBER 11**
The Corps begins a difficult crossing of the Bitterroot Mountains ; it takes 11 days, and leaves them nearly starved.

**NOVEMBER**
The Corps reaches the Pacific Ocean. Clark writes in his journal, "Ocian in view! Oh, the joy!"

**MARCH 23**
The Corps steal a Clatsop canoe and head up the Columbia River.

# INDEX